The Sun Rises and Falls in Southern Ontario

Photos by Gordon Rossignol, C.D.

To order additional copies of this book, contact:
Xlibris
1-888-795-4274
www.Xlibris.com
Orders@Xlibris.com

Contents
Sunrises

Contents
Sunsets

Gordon A. Rossignol, CD

I was born on September 15 in the year of our Lord 1960, in Toronto Ontario. I grew up like any other kid, playing outside having the wild fun of abandon and no responsibilities. At age 17 I started to get in to photography. Times were tough and I had to work so photography went out the window for a while and I started as a welder, school bus driver, labourer, joined the Windsor Regiment (reserves) twice; once in the late 70's for 2 years and again in the early 90's, 1993 till April 2005 when I did a component transfer to the regular force The Royal Canadian Dragoons for whom I worked till my medical release in April of 2012. I did half a tour in Afghanistan to replace a person who was rotated home. Due to a stupid accident caused by a superior I was injured and lost my hip two years later. I am now disabled and have gotten back into photography. I love sun sets and sun rises as well as a diverse field of interests. I hope you like and enjoy my book as much as I have enjoyed making it.

Thank You all very much
Gordon A. Rossignol, C.D., G.C.S., I.S.A.F.
R.C.D. Retired
High Speed Low Drag, Recce with a Punch

Gordon Rossignol, C.D

The Sun Rises and Falls in Southern Ontario

Gordon Rossignol, C.D

Gordon Rossignol, C.D

Gordon Rossignol, C.D

Gordon Rossignol, C.D

Gordon Rossignol, C.D

Gordon Rossignol, C.D

Gordon Rossignol, C.D

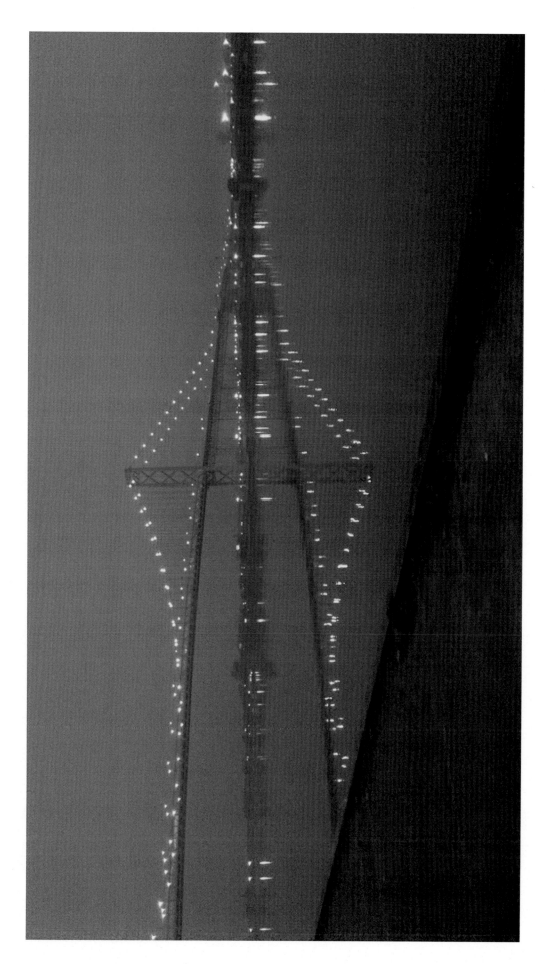

Gordon Rossignol, C.D

Gordon Rossignol, C.D

Gordon Rossignol, C.D

Gordon Rossignol, C.D

Gordon Rossignol, C.D

Gordon Rossignol, C.D

Gordon Rossignol, C.D

Gordon Rossignol, C.D

Gordon Rossignol, C.D

Gordon Rossignol, C.D

Gordon Rossignol, C.D

Gordon Rossignol, C.D

Gordon Rossignol, C.D

Gordon Rossignol, C.D

Gordon Rossignol, C.D

Gordon Rossignol, C.D

Gordon Rossignol, C.D

Printed in the United States
By Bookmasters